THE RUBÁIYÁT
OF
OMAR KHAYYAM

Rendered into English Verse
by Edward J. Fitzgerald

With Drawings by Edmund J. Sullivan

AIRMONT

AIRMONT PUBLISHING COMPANY, INC.
22 EAST 60TH STREET · NEW YORK 10022

An Airmont Classic

specially selected for the Airmont Library
from the immortal literature of the world

PRINTED IN THE UNITED STATES OF AMERICA

OMAR KHAYYÁM

THE ASTRONOMER-POET OF PERSIA

By Edward J. Fitzgerald

OMAR KHAYYÁM was born at Naishápúr in Khorassán in the
latter half of our Eleventh, and died within the First Quarter of our
Twelfth Century. The Slender Story of his Life is curiously
twined about that of two other very considerable Figures in their
Time and Country: one of whom tells the Story of all Three. This
was Nizám-ul-Mulk, Vizier to Alp Arslán the Son, and Malik Shah
the Grandson, of Toghrul Beg the Tartar, who had wrested Persia
from the feeble Successor of Mahmúd the Great, and founded
that Seljukian Dynasty which finally roused Europe into the Cru-
sades. This Nizám-ul-Mulk, in his. *Wasiyat*—or *Testament*—
which he wrote and left as a Memorial for future Statesmen—relates the following, as quoted in the *Calcutta Review*, No. 59,
from Mirkhond's History of the Assassins.

" 'One of the greatest of the wise men of Khorassán was the
Imám Mowaffak of Naishápúr, a man highly honored and rev-
erenced,—may God rejoice his soul; his illustrious years exceeded
eighty-five, and it was the universal belief that every boy who read
the Korán or studied the traditions in his presence, would assuredly
attain to honor and happiness. For this cause did my father send
me from Tús to Naishápúr with Abd-us-samad, the doctor of law,
that I might employ myself in study and learning under the guidance of that illustrious teacher. Towards me he ever turned an eye
of favor and kindness, and as his pupil I felt for him extreme affec-
tion and devotion, so that I passed four years in his service. When
I first came there, I found two other pupils of mine own age newly
arrived, Hakim Omar Khayyám, and the ill-fated Ben Sabbáh. Both
were endowed with sharpness of wit and the highest natural pow-
ers; and we three formed a close friendship together. When the
Imám rose from his lectures, they used to join me, and we re-
peated to each other the lessons we had heard. Now Omar was a
native of Naishápúr, while Hasan Ben Sabbáh's father was one Ali,
a man of austere life and practise, but heretical in his creed and
doctrine. One day Hasan said to me and to Khayyám, "It is a
universal belief that the pupils of the Imám Mowaffak will attain
to fortune. Now, even if we *all* do not attain thereto, without doubt
one of us will; what then shall be our mutual pledge and bond?"

3

Omar Khayyám

We answered, "Be it what you please." "Well," he said, "let us make a vow, that to whomsoever this fortune falls, he shall share it equally with the rest, and reserve no pre-eminence for himself." "Be it so," we both replied, and on those terms we mutually pledged our words. Years rolled on, and I went from Khorassán to Transoxiana, and wandered to Ghazni and Cabul; and when I returned, I was invested with office, and rose to be administrator of affairs during the Sultanate of Sultan Alp Arslán.'

"He goes on to state, that years passed by, and both his old school-friends found him out, and came and claimed a share in his good fortune, according to the school-day vow. The Vizier was generous and kept his word. Hasan demanded a place in the government, which the Sultan granted at the Vizier's request; but discontented with a gradual rise, he plunged into the maze of intrigue of an oriental court, and, failing in a base attempt to supplant his benefactor, he was disgraced and fell. After many mishaps and wanderings, Hasan became the head of the Persian sect of the *Ismailians*,—a party of fanatics who had long murmured in obscurity, but rose to an evil eminence under the guidance of his strong and evil will. In A.D. 1090, he seized the castle of Alamút, in the province of Rúdbar, which lies in the mountainous tract south of the Caspian Sea; and it was from this mountain home he obtained that evil celebrity among the Crusaders as the OLD MAN OF THE MOUNTAINS, and spread terror through the Mohammedan world; and it is yet disputed whether the word *Assassin*, which they have left in the language of modern Europe as their dark memorial, is derived from the *hashish*, or opiate of hempleaves (the Indian *bhang*), with which they maddened themselves to the sullen pitch of oriental desperation, or from the name of the founder of the dynasty, whom we have seen in his quiet collegiate days, at Naishápúr. One of the countless victims of the Assassin's dagger was Nizám-ul-Mulk himself, the old school-boy friend.[1]

[1] Some of Omar's Rubáiyát warn us of the danger of Greatness, the instability of Fortune, and while advocating Charity to all Men, recommending us to be too intimate with none, Attár makes Nizám-ul-Mulk use the very words of his friend Omar [Rub. xxviii], "When Nizám-ul-Mulk was in the Agony (of Death) he said, 'Oh God! I am passing away in the hand of the wind.'"

4

The Astronomer-Poet of Persia

"Omar Khayyám also came to the Vizier to claim his share; but not to ask for title or office. 'The greatest boon you can confer on me,' he said, 'is to let me live in a corner under the shadow of your fortune, to spread wide the advantages of Science, and pray for your long life and prosperity.' The Vizier tells us, that when he found Omar was really sincere in his refusal, he pressed him no further, but granted him a yearly pension of 1200 *mithkáls* of gold from the treasury of Naishápúr.

"At Naishápúr thus lived and died Omar Khayyám, 'busied,' adds the Vizier, 'in winning knowledge of every kind, and especially in Astronomy, wherein he attained to a very high preeminence. Under the Sultanate of Malik Shah, he came to Merv, and obtained great praise for his proficiency in science, and the Sultan showered favors upon him.'

"When the Malik Shah determined to reform the calendar, Omar was one of the eight learned men employed to do it; the result was the *Jaláli* era (so called from *Jalálud-din*, one of the king's names) —'a computation of time,' says Gibbon, 'which surpasses the Julian, and approaches the accuracy of the Gregorian style.' He is also the author of some astronomical tables, entitled 'Zíji-Malik-sháhí,' and the French have lately republished and translated an Arabic Treatise of his on Algebra.

"His Takhallus or poetical name (Khayyám) signifies a Tent-maker, and he is said to have at one time exercised that trade, perhaps before Nizám-ul-Mulk's generosity raised him to independence. Many Persian poets similarly derive their names from their occupations; thus we have Attár, 'a druggist,' Assár, 'an oil presser,' etc.[2] Omar himself alludes to his name in the following whimsical lines:—

" 'Khayyám, who stitched the tents of science,
    Has fallen in grief's furnace and been suddenly burned;
    The shears of Fate have cut the tent ropes of his life,
    And the broker of Hope has sold him for nothing!'

"We have only one more anecdote to give of his Life, and that relates to the close; it is told in the anonymous preface which is

---

[2] Through all these, like our Smiths, Archers, Millers, Fletchers, etc., may simply retain the Surname of an hereditary calling.

sometimes prefixed to his poems; it has been printed in the Persian in the Appendix to Hyde's *Veterum Persarum Religio,* p. 499; and D'Herbelot alludes to it in his Bibliothèque, under *Khiām.*

" 'It is written in the chronicles of the ancients that this King of the Wise, Omar Khayyám, died at Naishápúr in the year of the Hegira, 517 (A.D. 1123); in science he was unrivaled,—the very paragon of his age. Khwájah Nizámi of Samarcand, who was one of his pupils, relates the following story: "I often used to hold conversations with my teacher, Omar Khayyám, in a garden; and one day he said to me, 'My tomb shall be in a spot where the north wind may scatter roses over it.' I wondered at the words he spake, but I knew that his were no idle words.[8] Years after, when I chanced to revisit Naishápúr, I went to his final resting-place, and lo! it was just outside a garden, and trees laden with fruit stretched their boughs over the garden wall, and dropped their flowers upon his tomb, so that the stone was hidden under them." ' "

Thus far—without fear of Trespass—from the *Calcutta Review.* The writer of it, on reading in India this story of Omar's Grave, was reminded, he says, of Cicero's Account of finding Archimedes' Tomb at Syracuse, buried in grass and weeds. I think Thorwaldsen desired to have roses grow over him; a wish religiously fulfilled for him to the present day, I believe. However, to return to Omar.

Though the Sultan "shower'd Favors upon him," Omar's Epicurean Audacity of Thought and Speech caused him to be regarded askance in his Time and Country. He is said to have been especially hated and dreaded by the Súfis, whose Practise he ridiculed, and whose Faith amounts to little more than his own, when stript of the Mysticism and formal recognition of Islamism under which Omar would not hide. Their Poets, including Háfiz, who are (with the exception of Firdausi) the most considerable in Persia, borrowed largely, indeed, of Omar's material, but turning it to a mystical Use more convenient to Themselves and the People they addressed; a People quite as quick of Doubt as of Belief; as keen of Bodily sense as of Intellectual; and delighting in a cloudy composition of both, in which they could float luxuriously between

[8] The Rashness of the Words, according to D'Herbelot, consisted in being so opposed to those in the Korán: "No Man knows where he shall die."

Heaven and Earth, and this World and the Next, on the wings of a poetical expression, that might serve indifferently for either. Omar was too honest of Heart as well of Head for this. Having failed (however mistakenly) of finding any Providence but Destiny, and any World but This, he set about making the most of it; preferring rather to soothe the Soul through the Senses into Acquiescence with Things as he saw them, than to perplex it with vain disquietude after what they *might* be. It has been seen, however, that his Worldly Ambition was not exorbitant; and he very likely takes a humorous or perverse pleasure in exalting the gratification of Sense above that of the Intellect, in which he must have taken great delight, although it failed to answer the Questions in which he, in common with all men, was most vitally interested.

For whatever Reason, however, Omar as before said, has never been popular in his own Country, and therefore has been but scantily transmitted abroad. The MSS. of his Poems, mutilated beyond the average Casualties of Oriental Transcription, are so rare in the East as scarce to have reacht Westward at all, in spite of all the acquisitions of Arms and Science. There is no copy at the India House, none at the Bibliothèque Nationale of Paris. We know but of one in England: No. 140 of the Ouseley MSS. at the Bodleian, written at Shiráz, A.D. 1460. This contains but 158 Rubáiyát. One in the Asiatic Society's Library at Calcutta (of which we have a Copy), contains (and yet incomplete) 516, though swelled to that by all kinds of Repetition and Corruption. So Von Hammer speaks of *his* Copy as containing about 200, while Dr. Sprenger catalogues the Lucknow MS. at double that number.[4] The Scribes, too, of the Oxford and Calcutta MSS. seem to do their Work under a sort of Protest; each beginning with a tetrastich (whether genuine or not), taken out of its alphabetical order; the Oxford with one of Apology; the Calcutta with one of Expostulation, supposed (says a Notice prefixed to the MS.) to have arisen from a Dream, in which Omar's mother asked about his future fate. It may be rendered thus:—

[4] "Since this paper was written" (adds the Reviewer in a note), "we have met with a Copy of a very rare Edition, printed at Calcutta in 1836. This contains 438 Tetrastichs, with an Appendix containing 54 others not found in some MSS."

Omar Khayyám

"Oh Thou who burn'st in Heart for those who burn
In Hell, whose fires thyself shall feed in turn,
    How long be crying, 'Mercy on them, God!'
Why, who art Thou to teach, and He to learn?"

The Bodleian Quatrain pleads Pantheism by way of Justification.

    "If I myself upon a looser Creed
    Have loosely strung the Jewel of Good deed,
    Let this one thing for my Atonement plead:
    That One for Two I never did misread."

The Reviewer,[5] to whom I owe the Particulars of Omar's Life,
concludes his Review by comparing him with Lucretius, both as
to natural Temper and Genius, and as acted upon by the Circum-
stances in which he lived. Both indeed were men of subtle, strong,
and cultivated Intellect, fine Imagination, and Hearts passionate
for Truth and Justice; who justly revolted from their Country's
false Religion, and false, or foolish, Devotion to it; but who fell
short of replacing what they subverted by such better *Hope* as
others, with no better Revelation to guide them, had yet made a
Law to themselves. Lucretius indeed, with such material as
Epicurus furnished, satisfied himself with the theory of a vast
machine fortuitously constructed, and acting by a Law that implied
no Legislator; and so composing himself into a Stoical rather than
Epicurean severity of Attitude, sat down to contemplate the me-
chanical drama of the Universe which he was part Actor in; himself and all about him (as in his own sublime description of the
Roman Theater) discolored with the lurid reflex of the Curtain
suspended between the Spectator and the Sun. Omar, more desper-
ate, or more careless of any so complicated System as resulted in
nothing but hopeless Necessity, flung his own Genius and Learning with a bitter or humorous jest into the general Ruin which
their insufficient glimpses only served to reveal; and, pretending
sensual pleasure, as the serious purpose of Life, only *diverted*
himself with speculative problems of Deity, Destiny, Matter and
Spirit, Good and Evil, and other such questions, easier to start

[5] Professor Cowell.

than to run down, and the pursuit of which becomes a very weary sport at last!

With regard to the present Translation. The original Rubáiyát (as, missing an Arabic Guttural, these *Tetrastichs* are more musically called) are independent Stanzas, consisting each of four Lines of equal, though varied, Prosody; sometimes *all* rhyming, but oftener (as here imitated) the third line a blank. Somewhat as in the Greek Alcaic, where the penultimate line seems to lift and suspend the Wave that falls over in the last. As usual with such kind of Oriental Verse, the Rubáiyát follow one another according to Alphabetic Rhyme—a strange succession of Grave and Gay. Those here selected are strung into something of an Eclogue, with perhaps a less than equal proportion of the "Drink and make-merry," which (genuine or not) recurs over-frequently in the Original. Either way, the Result is sad enough: saddest perhaps when most ostentatiously merry: more apt to move Sorrow than Anger toward the old Tent-maker, who, after vainly endeavoring to unshackle his Steps from Destiny, and to catch some authentic Glimpse of To-MORROW, fell back upon To-DAY (which has outlasted so many To-morrows!) as the only Ground he had got to stand upon, however momentarily slipping from under his Feet.

I

Awake! for Morning in the Bowl of Night
Has flung the Stone that puts the Stars to Flight:
   And Lo! the Hunter of the East has caught
The Sultán's Turret in a Noose of Light.

I I

Dreaming when Dawn's Left Hand was in the Sky
I heard a Voice within the Tavern cry,
  "Awake, my Little ones, and fill the Cup
Before Life's Liquor in its Cup be dry."

III

And, as the Cock crew, those who stood before
The Tavern shouted—"Open then the Door.
  You know how little while we have to stay,
And, once departed, may return no more."

IV

Now the New Year reviving old Desires,
The thoughtful Soul to Solitude retires,
    Where the WHITE HAND OF MOSES on the
        Bough
Puts out, and Jesus from the Ground suspires.

V

Irám indeed is gone with all its Rose,
And Jamshýd's Sev'n-ring'd Cup where no one
     knows;
  But still the Vine her ancient Ruby yields,
And still a Garden by the Water blows.

VI

And David's Lips are lock't; but in divine
High piping Pélevi, with "Wine! Wine! Wine!
    Red Wine!"—the Nightingale cries to the Rose
That yellow Cheek of hers to'incarnadine.

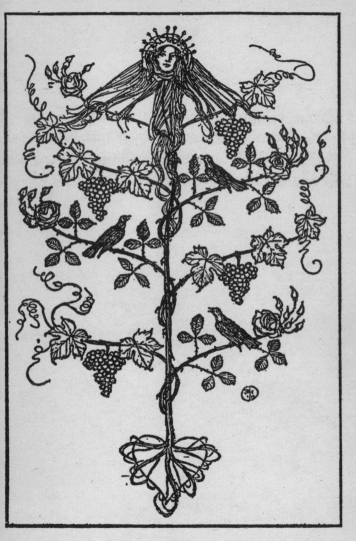

VII

Come, fill the Cup, and in the Fire of Spring
The Winter Garment of Repentance fling:
   The Bird of Time has but a little way
To fly—and Lo! the Bird is on the Wing.

VIII

And look—a thousand Blossoms with the Day
Woke—and a thousand scatter'd into Clay:
    And this first Summer Month that brings the
        Rose
Shall take Jamshyd and Kaikobád away.

IX

But come with old Khayyám, and leave the Lot
Of Kaikobád and Kaikhosrú forgot:
   Let Rustum lay about him as he will,
Or Hátim Tai cry Supper—heed them not.

X

With me along some Strip of Herbage strown
That just divides the desert from the sown,
  Where name of Slave and Sultán scarce is
    known,
And pity Sultán Máhmúd on his Throne.

XI

Here with a Loaf of Bread beneath the Bough,
A Flask of Wine, a Book of Verse—and Thou
   Beside me singing in the Wilderness—
And Wilderness is Paradise enow.

XII

"How sweet is mortal Sovranty!"—think some:
Others—"How blest the Paradise to come!"
    Ah, take the Cash in hand and waive the Rest;
Oh, the brave Music of a *distant* Drum!

XIII

Look to the Rose that blows about us—"Lo,
Laughing," she says, "into the World I blow:
  At once the silken Tassel of my Purse
Tear, and its Treasure on the Garden throw."

XIV

The Worldly Hope men set their Hearts upon
Turns Ashes—or it prospers; and anon,
    Like Snow upon the Desert's dusty Face
Lighting a little Hour or two—is gone.

XV

And those who husbanded the Golden Grain,
And those who flung it to the Winds like Rain,
   Alike to no such aureate Earth are turn'd
As, buried once, Men want dug up again.

XVI

Think, in this batter'd Caravanserai
Whose Doorways are alternate Night and Day,
    How Sultán after Sultán with his Pomp
Abode his Hour or two, and went his way.

XVII

They say the Lion and the Lizard keep
The Courts where Jamshyd gloried and drank
     deep:
  And Bahrám, that great Hunter—the Wild Ass
Stamps o'er his Head, and he lies fast asleep.

XVIII

I sometimes think that never blows so red
The Rose as where some buried Cæsar bled;
That every Hyacinth the Garden wears
Dropt in its Lap from some once lovely Head.

XIX

And this delightful Herb whose tender Green
Fledges the River's Lip on which we lean—
   Ah, lean upon it lightly! for who knows
From what once lovely Lip it springs unseen!

XX

Ah! my Belovéd, fill the Cup that clears
To-DAY of past Regrets and future Fears—
    To-morrow?—Why, To-morrow I may be
Myself with Yesterday's Sev'n Thousand Years.

XXI

Lo! some we loved, the loveliest and the best
That Time and Fate of all their Vintage prest,
    Have drunk their Cup a Round or two before
And one by one crept silently to Rest.

XXII

And we, that now make merry in the Room
They left, and Summer dresses in new Bloom,
    Ourselves must we beneath the Couch of Earth
Descend, ourselves to make a Couch—for whom?

XXIII

Ah, make the most of what we yet may spend,
Before we too into the Dust Descend;
    Dust into Dust, and under Dust, to lie,
Sans Wine, sans Song, sans Singer and—sans End!

XXIV

Alike for those who for TO-DAY prepare,
And those that after a TO-MORROW stare,
    A Muezzín from the Tower of Darkness cries
"Fools! your Reward is neither Here nor There."

XXV

Why, all the Saints and Sages who discuss'd
Of the Two Worlds so learnedly, are thrust
    Like foolish Prophets forth; their Words to
      Scorn
Are scatter'd, and their Mouths are stopt with
      Dust.

XXVI

Oh, come with old Khayyám, and leave the Wise
To talk; one thing is certain, that Life flies;
　　One thing is certain, and the Rest is Lies;
The Flower that once has blown for ever dies.

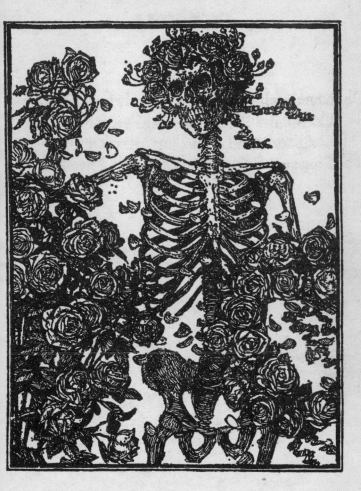

XXVII

Myself when young did eagerly frequent
Doctor and Saint, and heard great Argument
  About it and about: but evermore
Came out by the same Door as in I went.

XXVIII

With them the Seed of Wisdom did I sow,
And with my own hand labour'd it to grow:
   And this was all the Harvest that I reap'd—
"I came like Water, and like Wind I go."

XXIX

Into this Universe, and *why* not knowing,
Nor *whence*, like Water willy-nilly flowing:
   And out of it, as Wind along the Waste,
I know not *whither*, willy-nilly blowing.

XXX

What, without asking, hither hurried *whence?*
And, without asking, *whither* hurried hence!
    Another and another Cup to drown
The Memory of this Impertinence!

XXXI

Up from Earth's Centre through the seventh Gate
I rose, and on the Throne of Saturn sate,
    And many Knots unravel'd by the Road;
But not the Knot of Human Death and Fate.

XXXII

There was a Door to which I found no Key:
There was a Veil past which I could not see:
    Some little Talk awhile of Me and Thee
There seemed—and then no more of Thee and
    Me.

XXXIII

Then to the rolling Heav'n itself I cried,
Asking, "What Lamp had Destiny to guide
    Her little Children stumbling in the Dark?"
And—"A blind understanding!" Heav'n replied.

XXXIV

Then to this earthen Bowl did I adjourn
My Lip the secret Well of Life to learn:
 And Lip to Lip it murmur'd—"While you live,
Drink!—for once dead you never shall return."

XXXV

I think the Vessel, that with fugitive
Articulation answer'd, once did live,
    And merry-make; and the cold Lip I kiss'd
How many Kisses might it take—and give.

XXXVI

For in the Market-place, one Dusk of Day,
I watch'd the Potter thumping his wet Clay:
  And with its all obliterated Tongue
It murmur'd—"Gently, Brother, gently, pray!"

XXXVII

One Moment in Annihilation's Waste,
One moment, of the Well of Life to taste—
    The Stars are setting, and the Caravan
Starts for the dawn of Nothing—Oh, make haste!

XXXVIII

Ah, fill the Cup:—what boots it to repeat
How Time is slipping underneath our Feet:
   Unborn To-MORROW and dead YESTERDAY,
Why fret about them if To-DAY be sweet!

XXXIX

How long, how long, in infinite Pursuit
Of This and That endeavour and dispute?
    Better be merry with the fruitful Grape
Than sadden after none, or bitter, Fruit.

XL

You know, my Friends, how long since in my
       House
For a new Marriage I did make Carouse:
   Divorced old barren Reason from my Bed,
And took the Daughter of the Vine to Spouse.

XLI

For "Is" and "Is-not" though *with* Rule and Line,
And, "Up-and-Down" *without*, I could define,
   I yet in all I only cared to know,
Was never deep in anything but—Wine.

XLII

And lately, by the Tavern Door agape,
Came stealing through the Dusk an Angel Shape,
　　Bearing a vessel on his Shoulder; and
He bid me taste of it; and 'twas—the Grape!

XLIII

The Grape that can with Logic absolute
The Two-and-Seventy jarring Sects confute:
   The subtle Alchemist that in a Trice
Life's leaden Metal into Gold transmute.

XLIV

The mighty Mahmúd, the victorious Lord,
That all the misbelieving and black Horde
   Of Fears and Sorrows that infest the Soul
Scatters and slays with his enchanted Sword.

XLV

But leave the Wise to wrangle, and with me
The Quarrel of the Universe let be:
   And, in some corner of the Hubbub coucht,
Make Game of that which makes as much of
     Thee.

XLVI

For in and out, above, about, below,
'Tis nothing but a Magic Shadow-show,
   Play'd in a Box whose Candle is the Sun,
Round which we Phantom Figures come and go

XLVII

And if the Wine you drink, the Lip you press,
End in the Nothing all Things end in—Yes—
    Then fancy while Thou art, Thou art but what
Thou shalt be—Nothing—Thou shalt not be less.

XLVIII

While the Rose blows along the River Brink,
With old Khayyám the Ruby Vintage drink:
   And when the Angel with his darker Draught
Draws up to thee—take that, and do not shrink.

XLIX

'Tis all a Chequer-board of Nights and Days
Where Destiny with Men for Pieces plays:
    Hither and thither moves, and mates, and slays,
And one by one back in the Closet lays.

L

The Ball no Question makes of Ayes and Noes,
But Right or Left as strikes the Player goes;
    And He that toss'd Thee down into the Field,
He knows about it all—HE knows—HE knows!

LI

The Moving Finger writes; and, having writ,
Moves on: nor all thy Piety nor Wit
    Shall lure it back to cancel half a Line,
Nor all thy Tears wash out a Word of it.

LII

And that inverted Bowl we call The Sky,
Whereunder crawling coop't we live and die,
   Lift not thy hands to *It* for help—for It
Rolls impotently on as Thou or I.

LIII

With Earth's first Clay They did the Last Man's
 knead,
And then of the Last Harvest sow'd the Seed:
 Yea, the first Morning of Creation wrote
What the Last Dawn of Reckoning shall read.

LIV

I tell Thee this—When, starting from the Goal,
Over the shoulders of the flaming Foal
    Of Heav'n Parwín and Mushtarí they flung,
In my predestin'd Plot of Dust and Soul.

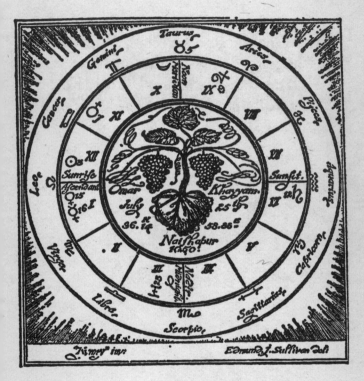

LV

The Vine had struck a Fibre; which about
It clings my Being—let the Súfi flout;
   Of my Base Metal may be filed a Key,
That shall unlock the Door he howls without.

LVI

And this I know: whether the one True Light,
Kindle to Love, or Wrath consume me quite,
    One Glimpse of It within the Tavern caught
Better than in the Temple lost outright.

LVII

Oh Thou who didst with Pitfall and with Gin
Beset the Road I was to wander in,
    Thou wilt not with Predestination round
Enmesh me, and impute my Fall to Sin?

LVIII

Oh Thou, who Man of baser Earth didst make,
And who with Eden didst devise the Snake;
   For all the Sin wherewith the Face of Man
Is blacken'd, Man's Forgiveness give—and take!

*   *   *   *   *

LIX

KUZA—NÁMA

Listen again. One Evening at the Close
Of Ramazán, ere the better Moon arose,
 In that old Potter's Shop I stood alone
With the clay Population round in Rows.

LX

And strange to tell, among that Earthen Lot
Some could articulate, while others not:
    And suddenly one more impatient cried—
"Who *is* the Potter, pray, and who the Pot?"

LXI

Then said another—"Surely not in vain
My substance from the common Earth was ta'en,
  That He who subtly wrought me into Shape
Should stamp me back to common Earth again."

LXII

Another said—"Why, ne'er a peevish Boy
Would break the Bowl from which he drank in
    Joy;
  Shall He that *made* the Vessel in pure Love
And Fansy, in an after Rage destroy!"

LXIII

None answer'd this; but after Silence spake
A Vessel of a more ungainly Make:
   "They sneer at me for leaning all awry;
What? did the Hand then of the Potter shake?"

LXIV

Said one—"Folks of a surly Tapster tell,
And daub his Visage with the Smoke of Hell;
    They talk of some strict Testing of us—Pish!
He's a Good Fellow, and 'twill all be well."

EDMUND J SULLIVAN

LXV

Then said another with a long-drawn Sigh,
"My Clay with long oblivion is gone dry:
    But, fill me with the old familiar Juice,
Methinks I might recover by-and-bye!"

LXVI

So, while the Vessels one by one were speaking,
One spied the little Crescent all were seeking:
    And then they jogg'd each other, "Brother!
        Brother!
Hark to the Porter's Shoulder-knot a-creaking!"

      *   *   *   *   *

LXVII

Ah, with the Grape my fading Life provide,
And wash my Body whence the life has died,
   And in a Windingsheet of Vineleaf wrapt,
So bury me by some sweet Gardenside.

LXVIII

That ev'n my buried Ashes such a Snare
Of Perfume shall fling up into the Air,
    As not a True Believer passing by
But shall be overtaken unaware. .

LXIX

Indeed, the Idols I have loved so long
Have done my Credit in Men's Eye much wrong:
    Have drown'd my Honour in a shallow Cup,
And sold my Reputation for a Song.

LXX

Indeed, indeed, Repentance oft before
I swore—but was I sober when I swore?
    And then and then came Spring, and Rose-in-
      hand
My thread-bare Penitence a-pieces tore.

LXXI

And much as Wine has play'd the Infidel,
And robb'd me of my Robe of Honour—well
   I often wonder what the Vintners buy
One half so precious as the Goods they sell.

· LXXII

Alas, that Spring should vanish with the Rose!
That Youth's sweet-scented Manuscript should
    close!
  The Nightingale that in the Branches sang,
Ah, whence, and whither flown again, who knows!

LXXIII

Ah, Love! could thou and I with Fate conspire
To grasp this sorry Scheme of Things entire,
  Would not we shatter it to bits—and then
Re-mould it nearer to the Heart's Desire!

LXXIV

Ah, Moon of my Delight who know'st no wane,
The Moon of Heav'n is rising once again:
  How oft hereafter rising shall she look
Through this same Garden after me—in vain!

LXXV

And when Thyself with shining Foot shall pass
Among the Guests Star-scattere'd on The Grass,
  And in Thy joyous Errand reach the Spot
Where I made one—turn down an empty Glass!

TAMÁM SHUD.